Sentence Correction 2

Chad Troutwine · Markus Moberg · Mark Glenn · Brian Galvin · Cliff Smith

Co-Founders	Chad Troutwine
	Markus Moberg
Senior Managing Editor	Mark Glenn
Director of Academic Programs	Brian Galvin
Interior Design	Miriam Lubow
	Lisa Johnson
Cover Design	Nick Mason
	Mike Miller
Contributing Editors	Jim Stekelberg
	Joseph Dise
	Tatiana Becker
	Jasun Sun
Contributing Writers	Chris Kane
	Jim Stekelberg
	Neil Moakley
	Christopher Laconi
Lesson Ideas	George Yates

A successful educational program is only as good as the people who teach it, and Veritas Prep is fortunate to have many of the world's finest GMAT instructors on its team.

Not only does that team know how to teach a strong curriculum, but it also knows how to help create one. This lesson book would not be possible without the hundreds of suggestions we have received from our talented faculty all across the world— from Seattle, Detroit, and Miami to London, Singapore, and Dubai. Their passion for excellence helped give birth to a new curriculum that is far better than what we could have created on our own.

Our students also deserve a very special thanks. Thousands of them have provided us with something priceless: enthusiastic feedback that has guided us in creating the most comprehensive GMAT preparation course available on the market today.

We therefore dedicate this revised lesson book to all Veritas Prep instructors and students who have tackled the GMAT and given us their valuable input along the way.

Table of Contents

Lesson 11 Introduction

Sentence Correction intimidates many students because at first blush it appears to encompass an enormous range of topics within the English language. In fact, the number of grammatical issues covered is quite limited. Through exhaustive research, we have gathered and categorized all Sentence Correction errors under a single system, VAMPIRES. In Sentence Correction 1, you learned the Veritas methodology for catching these errors. This lesson builds on those insights. Today we will cover some of the trickier error subtypes so that you will know how to catch every error that might appear on the test.

Sentence Correction 2

In the Sentence Correction 1 lesson, you learned to use the powerful VAMPIRES checklist to identify and eliminate grammatical errors. You should attack any Sentence Correction question through the lens of VAMPIRES, proactively "seeking and destroying" the errors you know to be prevalent on the exam.

In the Sentence Correction 2 lesson, you will receive more practice with VAMPIRES, as well as take a closer look at some of the finer points of a few of these error categories. As promised, we will spend more time on common Idiomatic errors, as well as deconstruct some of the more intricate grammatical devices that comprise the VAMPIRES categories The topics you will cover in this lesson include:

•   A closer look at … Verb Form

•   A closer look at … Agreement

•   A closer look at … Modifiers

•   A closer look at … Idioms

•   A closer look at … Second-Tier Errors

Throughout the lesson and the problems that follow, you will have opportunities to hone your skills with the VAMPIRES errors; remember, most sentence correction questions feature more than one error category.

A closer look at ... Verb Form: Additional Dimensions

Verbs have at least four dimensions which the writer can use to convey his or her thoughts. The first two dimensions are part of the tense.

Time frame: past, present, or future

Aspect: simple, perfect / complete, or continuous / progressive

GMAT Insider: The passive voice is less preferable than the active voice and is often (but not always) part of an incorrect answer choice (a Second-Tier-Fluency error) on the GMAT.

Recall from Sentence Correction 1 some possible combinations of time frame and aspect—

Example of the simple past tense: I studied.
Example of the past perfect tense: I had studied.
Example of the past continuous tense: I was studying.

Most verb form errors will appear in the form of incorrect tense or aspect. Some, however, may include the lesser-tested dimensions below.

A third dimension of verb usage is **voice**: active or passive.
In the active voice, the subject *performs* the action.
In the passive voice, the subject *receives* the action. Verbs in passive voice always include some form of the verb *be* (such as *be, is, are, was, were,* or *been*).

Example of the active voice: I found the discrepancy.
Example of the passive voice: A mistake was made.

A fourth dimension of verb usage is **mood**: indicative, imperative, or subjunctive
The mood conveys the writer's attitude about the statement.

The indicative mood is by far the most commonly used. The indicative mood is used to express facts and opinions, and conveys a definite attitude.

Example of the indicative mood: He goes to the library often.

The imperative mood is used to give orders or to make requests. The imperative is identical to the second person indicative (but the subject "you" is left unstated).

Example of the imperative mood: Go to the library and check out that book.

The subjunctive mood is seldom used, but is required in some specific circumstances, such as in clauses after certain verbs.

Example of the subjunctive mood: I wish that you were here.

Subjunctive Mood

The subjunctive mood is infrequently used and is – in many cases – identical to the indicative. As a result, you may not be aware when you use the subjunctive (automatically and unconsciously).

For **regular verbs**, the present tense subjunctive is identical to the first person singular of the indicative. In the indicative mood, only the third person singular differs from the first person singular, so the subjunctive is only evident in the third person singular:

		Indicative mood	Subjunctive mood
Singular	1st person	study	study
	2nd person	study	study
	3rd person	studies	study
Plural	1st person	study	study
	2nd person	study	study
	3rd person	study	study

For regular verbs, the past tense subjunctive is always identical to the past tense indicative (*studied*).

The verb *to be* is highly irregular in both indicative and subjunctive moods.

		Present tense		Past tense	
		Indicative mood	Subjunctive mood	Indicative mood	Subjunctive mood
Singular	1st person	am	be	was	were
	2nd person	are	be	were	were
	3rd person	is	be	was	were
Plural	1st person	are	be	were	were
	2nd person	are	be	were	were
	3rd person	are	be	were	were

The subjunctive mood is required in three types of statements:

1. In dependent clauses **after verbs that express demands** or recommendations. Such "demanding" verbs include ask, command, demand, order, recommend, require, suggest, and urge.

Example: *The president demanded that the senator <u>explain</u> the effects of the bill.*

2. In dependent clauses **after an adjective that expresses urgency.** Adjectives expressing urgency include crucial, essential, important, imperative, necessary, and urgent.

Example: *It is crucial that a student <u>prepare</u> properly for the GMAT.*

3. In clauses that express situations that are **hypothetical or contrary-to-fact.** For an if clause that expresses a hypothetical situation in the present or future, use a time-shift subjunctive.

Time-shift Subjunctives

Indicative mood	Subjunctive mood
am / is / are	were
studied	had studied

For a consequence clause (after an if clause), use the **conditional** form of the verb (containing *would, could or might or, less frequently,* should).

Example: *If I <u>were</u> king, lawyers <u>would be</u> outlawed.*

Dependent clauses after the verb *wish* express hypothetical situations; use the time-shift subjunctive in such cases.

Example: *I wish that you <u>were</u> here.*

1.	Many companies <u>require that every employee be reviewed by his or her superior</u> twice a year.

(A)	require that every employee be reviewed by his or her superior

(B)	require that every employee to be reviewed by his or her superior

(C)	require that every employee will be reviewed by his or her superior

(D)	have a requirement for an employee review

(E)	have a requirement to review every employee

A closer look at … Agreement

As you learned in Sentence Correction 1, subject-verb agreement is a relatively simple concept, but is also one that is relatively simple for the GMAT to obscure. Through the use of multiple nouns, lengthy modifying clauses, and inverted subject-verb orders, the writers of the GMAT can entice you toward incorrect answer choices, as you have undoubtedly seen in your homework and practice tests thus far.

Another device that the GMAT writers employ to add difficulty to Agreement errors is the use of tricky subjects – those that you may not automatically recognize to be singular or plural. Consider the following drill:

Agreement Drill

Try to determine whether the following subjects are singular or plural:

1. Anyone…

2. Everyone…

3. A group of soldiers…

4. The running of the bulls…

5. Bob and his mother…

6. Velma, along with her mother,…

7. One or both of us…

8. Neither Greek nor Latin…

9. Whoever…

10. No one…

11. The home team…

12. Each of the students…

13. The number of men…

14. A number of women…

15. Alcott's *Little Women*…

Note
Confusing subjects are more often singular than plural.

Collective nouns are nouns that refer to a group but are in fact singular. Examples of collective nouns include *group* and *team* from #3 and #11 above. Other examples are *audience* and *crowd*.

Indefinite pronouns are pronouns, like *anyone* or *whoever* from #1 and #9 above, that don't refer to anything specific. All indefinite pronouns are singular, with the exception of **SANAM** pronouns, which may be singular or plural, and are not tested on the GMAT.

Remember the Slash and Burn strategy for Agreement errors: first, cut out the words between subject and verb to determine the simple subject, and second, match the simple subject up with the verb.

Note

SANAM pronouns are the one exception to this rule. When the simple subject is *some, any, none, all,* or *most,* you must also look at the *of* phrase that follows (if it exists). If the word following "of" is singular, the subject is singular; if it is plural, the subject is plural. Again, SANAM pronouns are not tested on the GMAT.

Agreement Between Nouns

Normally when we talk about agreement we are referring to one of two things: agreement between subject and verb, or agreement between pronoun and antecedent. However, there are also some circumstances where two nouns must agree with each other.

Example: The soldiers will take on tasks such as supplying the front lines and acting as a guard.

Corrected: The soldiers will take on tasks such as supplying the front lines and acting as guards.

Because the soldiers are individually acting as guards, *guards* must agree in number with *soldiers* – just like a pronoun must agree with its antecedent.

2.   <u>A newly discovered letter by Jonathan Swift, written in the same year as *Gulliver's Travels* were published</u>, shows how the biting satire that marked many of Swift's public works was reflected in his private writings as well.

(A)   A newly discovered letter by Jonathan Swift, written in the same year as *Gulliver's Travels* were published,

(B)   A newly discovered letter by Jonathan Swift, written in the same year of publication as *Gulliver's Travels*,

(C)   A newly discovered letter by Jonathan Swift, written in the same year that *Gulliver's Travels* was published,

(D)   Jonathan Swift wrote a newly discovered letter in the same year as he published *Gulliver's Travels* that

(E)   Jonathan Swift wrote a newly discovered letter in the same year of publication as *Gulliver's Travels* that

A closer look at ... Modifiers

As you learned in Sentence Correction 1, a modifier error occurs when the modifier does not modify what it is supposed to. While modifiers can be either adverbial (modifying the action of the sentence) or adjectival (modifying a noun), the vast majority of modifier errors on the GMAT involve adjectival modifiers. There are three distinct classes of adjectival modifiers that you may find on the GMAT. While ultimately your job remains to determine simply whether the modifier accurately modifies what it is supposed to, a more in-depth understanding of each type may make that job easier to perform. The three types of adjectival modifiers are:

Participial Phrases, Appositive Phrases, and Relative Clauses

Participial Phrases

A participle is a verb form used as an adjective.

Examples:
*The **crying** baby finally fell asleep.*

***Smiling**, the woman left the room.*

*The **wrecked** car was sent to the salvage yard.*

What is a participial phrase? It is a longer modifying phrase starting with a participle.

Examples:
***Bombarded by bullets**, the troops retreated.*

*Dogs **trained by professionals** are much more obedient.*

*Kit Carson roamed the Rockies and the Southwest, **working as a trapper and establishing a reputation as one of the most able mountain men of his time.***

The rules for participial phrases are relatively straightforward:

1.   If you start a sentence with a participial phrase, it must always logically modify the noun that follows the comma. Example of a modifier error of this type:

Error: *Alarmed by the recent decline of the stock market, many retirement investments have been switched from stocks to more conservative options, such as money market funds.*

Corrected: *Alarmed by the recent decline of the stock market,* many investors have switched their retirement investments from stocks to more conservative options, such as money market funds.

2.   If participial phrases are used in the middle of a sentence, they follow the noun they are modifying and are either set off by commas or not, depending on whether the information is essential to the meaning of the sentence.

Examples:
Dogs trained by professionals are generally very obedient.
(Essential to the meaning of the sentence so no commas.)

The city's oldest church, **recently destroyed by fire,** *has not yet been rebuilt.*
(Extra, non-essential information so commas must be used)

Error: *Children, introduced to music early, develop strong intellectual skills.*

Corrected: *Children introduced to music early develop strong intellectual skills.*

3.   When participial phrases are put at the end of a sentence with a comma, they are confusing because they can modify the subject of the sentence or clause preceding it even though they are not beside it. Consider the previous example:

Kit Carson roamed the Rockies and the Southwest, **working as a trapper and establishing a reputation as one of the most able mountain men of his time.**

This might appear to be an error of modification or parallelism to many students. However, the participial phrases at the end are properly modifying Kit Carson, even though the modifiers are very far away from the noun they are modifying. Because this is a confusing construction for many test-takers, it is used frequently on the GMAT.

> *GMAT Insider:* While most adjectival modifiers should be beside the noun they are modifying, participial phrases can be far from the noun they are modifying when attached with a comma at the end of a sentence or clause.

3.   Originally called 'BackRub', the founders of Google were two Stanford PhD students, Sergey Brin and Larry Page, whose father, Dr. Carl Victor Page, earned his doctorate in computer science from the University of Michigan.

(A)   Originally called 'BackRub', the founders of Google were two Stanford PhD students, Sergey Brin and Larry Page, whose father, Dr. Carl Victor Page, earned his doctorate in computer science from the University of Michigan

(B)   Originally called "BackRub", two Stanford PhD students, Sergey Brin and Larry Page, whose father, Dr. Carl Victor Page, earned his doctorate in computer science from the University of Michigan, were the founders of Google

(C)   Originally called "BackRub", Google was founded by two Stanford PhD students, Larry Page, whose father, Dr. Carl Victor Page, earned his doctorate in computer science from the University of Michigan, and Sergey Brin

(D)   Google was founded by two Stanford PhD students, Sergey Brin and Larry Page, whose father, Dr. Carl Victor Page, earned his doctorate in computer science from the University of Michigan, and was originally called "BackRub"

(E)   The founders being two Stanford PhD students, Sergey Brin and Larry Page, whose father, Dr. Carl Victor Page, earned his doctorate in computer science from the University of Michigan, Google was originally called "BackRub"

Appositive Phrases

Despite the technical name, these phrases are fairly easy to understand and very common in the English language. An appositive phrase is simply a noun phrase that serves the role of an adjective.

Examples:
*John, **the lead singer of the band**, has laryngitis.*

***A gifted student and talented musician**, John graduated from USC with highest honors.*

*John spent last weekend visiting USC, **his alma mater.***

As you might notice, these modifiers are almost always non-essential information so they need to be set off by commas. Basically, the rules that govern appositive phrases are the same rules that you learned for participial phrases. The only difference is that appositive modifiers cannot be far away from the noun they are modifying.

Note
Appositive phrases are often used to confuse students for subject verb agreement or simply to make a sentence more complicated. If they are not part of what is being tested in the problem, simply remove them using slash and burn to simplify the sentence.

> *Habits of Great Test Takers:* Sign up for the GMAT right now! Not only is necessity the mother of invention, but having a deadline will help you to focus your efforts. The worst thing you could do is to wait until you are "ready" to sign up for the GMAT. Setting a deadline will force you to get ready.
>
> - Aaron Pond, SALT LAKE CITY

4.   Politicians and philosophers, <u>early forms of democratic government and public discourse were pioneered by the ancient Greeks, laying the groundwork for much of modern society.</u>

(A)   early forms of democratic government and public discourse were pioneered by the ancient Greeks, laying the groundwork for much of modern society

(B)   laying the groundwork for much of modern society, early forms of democratic government and public discourse were pioneered by the ancient Greeks

(C)   the ancient Greeks pioneered early forms of democratic government and public discourse, laying the groundwork for much of modern society

(D)   there were pioneered, laying the groundwork for much of modern society, early forms of democratic government and public discourse by the ancient Greeks

(E)   were the ancient Greeks who, laying the groundwork for much of modern society, pioneered early forms of democratic government and public discourse

Relative Clauses

What is a relative clause? It is a subordinate clause that starts with a relative pronoun and is used to modify a noun. The most common relative pronouns that start a relative clause are:

Who, Which, That, Where, Whose, Whom

Examples of relative clauses:
*The boy **who lives next door** is my friend.*   (Essential information so comma is not used)

*Susan, **who lives next doo**r, is coming to the party.* (Non-essential information so comma must be used)

*The dog **that Bill found** belongs to my neighbor.* (Essential information so comma is not used)

*My car, **which breaks down regularly**, has become expensive to own. (Non-essential information so comma must be used)*

The most common mistakes relating to relative clauses take place when they are used to modify action in a sentence or when they are placed too far from the noun they are modifying.

Error: It rained yesterday, which forced me to cancel the event.

Corrected: It rained yesterday, and as a result I was forced to cancel the event.

Error: The deposit that I put on the house, which is non-refundable, is in jeopardy if I cannot get financing.

Corrected: The non-refundable deposit that I put on the house is in jeopardy if I cannot get financing.

IMPORTANT STRATEGY TIP: When you see a relative clause in any GMAT Sentence Correction problem, simply look at the noun before the relative pronoun and ask: Is this logically modified by the relative clause? If there is no noun or the relative clause does not properly modify the noun then it is an error. While there are exceptions to this (relative clauses can sometimes modify nouns that are not directly beside them) you should not worry about them for GMAT Sentence Correction.

5.   The economic report released today by Congress and the Federal Reserve was
        bleaker than expected, <u>which suggests that the nearing recession might be even
        deeper and more prolonged than even the most pessimistic analysts have
        predicted</u>

(A)   which suggests that the nearing recession might be even deeper and more
        prolonged than even the most pessimistic analysts have predicted.

(B)   which suggests that the nearing recession might be deeper and more
        prolonged than that predicted by even the most pessimistic analysts.

(C)   suggests that the nearing recession might be even deeper and more prolonged
        than that predicted by even the most pessimistic analysts.

(D)   suggesting that the nearing recession might be deeper and more prolonged
        than that predicted by even the most pessimistic analysts.

(E)   a situation that is even more deep and prolonged than even the most
        pessimistic analysts have predicted.

A closer look at … Idioms

Idiomatic errors are likely the most difficult to study, as the English language is full of obscure and confusing rules. Quite literally, there are many idioms regarding which English majors and newspaper editors feel unsure; a classic "cop-out" employed by almost all writers is the notion that "when in doubt, find another way to write it so that you don't have to worry". Unfortunately, in the context of a multiple-choice test, you won't be able to rewrite around idioms that trouble you, but you do have some tools at your disposal to help you navigate the murky waters surrounding idioms on the GMAT.

In addition to the strategies you learned for Idioms in the Sentence Correction 1 lesson, note that:

1)   The GMAT tests several recurring idioms that can be categorized (and will be categorized in this lesson)

2)   Idioms on the GMAT are quite often smokescreens, and you can avoid them by looking for other VAMPIRES errors first (the classic editorial "cop-out")

To start, let's look at a problem that features a relatively unique idiom:

6. Many professional football teams have found that <u>they are better served by selecting linemen in the college draft instead of selecting</u> skill position players such as wide receivers or quarterbacks, who tend to demand higher salaries and who take longer to develop into quality players at the professional level.

(A) they are better served by selecting linemen in the college draft instead of selecting

(B) selecting linemen in the college draft better serves them than the selection of

(C) they are better served by selecting linemen in the college draft rather than by selecting

(D) the selection of linemen is better than

(E) they are better served by selecting linemen in the college draft than by selecting

The instead of vs. rather than idiom is a unique one, and one that doesn't belong to a particular category that would aid your study. For the sake of accuracy:

"Instead of" is used when an item simply takes the place of another. An example:

May I please have coffee instead of orange juice?

Here, one beverage replaces another, and "instead of" translates to "in place of", connoting a one-for-one substitution.

"Rather than" is used to denote preference. An example:

I would rather have coffee than orange juice. OR I would like to have coffee rather than orange juice.

As you can see, instead of vs. rather than is an extremely subtle distinction, and accordingly is one on which you could expend quite a bit of time and energy. As a savvy test taker, however, you know that it is best to save idioms for last, and to first look for other errors. In doing so, you would have found the Rudimentary Sentence error in this question, and avoided the tedious idiomatic evaluation altogether.

Commonly-occurring Idiom Categories

Naturally, you will not be able to simply avoid all idiomatic decisions on the GMAT, but many that you will be forced to handle are members of distinct categories which can help you prioritize your study. These categories include:

Countable vs. Uncountable (a variation of singular vs. plural)

A common Idiom error relates to the concept of "countability" or whether a noun is treated as singular (it cannot be counted) or plural (it can be counted). Some nouns, like sand, are considered to be uncountable, and therefore taken as a singular entity. Other nouns, like grains, are taken as plural because we recognize – and could theoretically count – them as individuals.

Example of a Countability Error: This line is for customers with ten items or less

The same sentence, corrected: This line is for customers with ten items or fewer ("items" is plural, and can be counted, so we must use "fewer" instead of "less")

The following table shows the designation between the modifiers used for "countable" and "uncountable" nouns:

Countable	Uncountable
Number	Amount
Many	Much
Few	Little
Fewer	Less
Several	Some

One vs. Two vs. More-than-two

Another type of Idiom error relates to the use of adjectives and adverbs that describe differing numbers of items. When one thing is described, use the positive (simple) form:

Correct Examples: *My team is strong. Your team performed poorly.*

When two things are being compared with an adjective or adverb, use the comparative form of the adjective/adverb.

Correct Examples: *My team is stronger than yours. Your team performed more poorly than mine.*

When more than two things are being compared, use the superlative form.

Correct Examples: *My team is the strongest in the league. Your team performed the most poorly on Sunday.*

> *GMAT Insider*: The GMAT will not expect you to know whether a word uses a regular or irregular form. However, it will expect you to know whether to use the positive, comparative, or superlative form.

Adjective and Adverb Forms

	Positive	Comparative	Superlative
Regular	Fast	Faster	Fastest
	Easy	Easier	Easiest
	Tall	Taller	Tallest
	Etc	Etc. +er	Etc. + est
Regular	Right	More Right	Most Right
	Happily	More Happily	Most Happily
	Energetically	More Energetically	Most Energetically
	Etc.	More + Etc.	Most + Etc.
Irregular	Good	Better	Best
	Bad	Worse	Worst
	Little	Less/Lesser	Least
	Much/Many	More	Most
	Far	Farther/Further	Farthest/Furthest
	Late	Later/Latter	Latest/Last
	Old	Older/Elder	Oldest/Eldest

Other Idioms pertain to the comparison of two items vs. the comparison of three-or-more items. These include:

Two	More-than-Two
Between*	Among
The other	Another
Each other	One another

An easy way to remember the latter two distinctions is to consider the word "another" to be a combination of "any other", signifying that there are multiple "others".

Examples:
Sustainable energy has been a topic of discussion among the European leaders.

Between you and me, I think it is a good idea.

Arnold Schwarzenegger and Danny DeVito do not look anything like each other.

Everybody get together to try to love one another.

*Please note: As is common in the English language, there are some exceptions to the rule when it comes to the use of "between". The GMAT, however, has traditionally only tested the concept as it is presented above.

Comparison Idioms

As you learned in Sentence Correction 1, sentences that feature comparisons are likely to contain idiomatic errors. Those that do will typically do so by jumbling the common idiomatic expressions in the vertical columns below.

As	So	More/Less
Many/Much		
As	That	Than

7.   Of all the events leading to the formation of the Earth, the catalyst for the infinite mass of matter that caused the Big Bang <u>is maybe the more difficult for determination</u>.

(A)   is maybe the more difficult for determination

(B)   is probably the most difficult to determine

(C)   is maybe the most difficult for determination

(D)   is probably the more difficult to determine

(E)   is, it may be, the determination that is most difficult

Popular GMAT Idioms

In Sentence Correction I, you learned that idiomatic errors often appear on the verbal portion of the GMAT. Unfortunately, there are literally thousands of possible idioms that could be tested. Obviously we cannot cover every idiom, but we have listed some of the most common (the * denotes elements that must be parallel):

Ability to
Agree with (a person or concept)
X* as an instance of y*
As many x as y
Attend to (someone)
Based on
Between x* and y*
Centers on
Conform to
Contrast x* with y*
Credit x with y
Defined as
Depicted as
Distinguish between x* and y*
Doubt that
Enable to
Fascinated by
For every x*, y*
Identical with
Indifferent towards
Just as x*, so y*
Mistake x* for y*
(No) more x* than y*/(no) less x* than y*
More x* than y*
Not x*, but rather y*
Not so much x* as y*
Order that x be y/order x to be y
Prohibit x from y
Range from x* to y*
Regard as
Require x to y
Responsible for
Result in
Retroactive to
Sequence of
So x that y
Substitute x* for y*
The same to x* as to y*
Unlike x*, y*

Agree on/to (a deal or plan)
X* as a means to y*
As x as y
As much as
Attribute x to y/x is attributed to y
Believe x* to be y*
Both x* and y*
Concerned with
Consider x y
Created with
A debate over
Depends on whether
Different from/differ from
Distinguish x* from y*
Either x* or y*
Estimate to be
Forbid x to do y
From x* to y*
In contrast to
X* is more than y*
Like x*, y*
Modeled after
More… than ever
Neither x* nor y*
Not only x* but also y*
Order x to y
Probably not x*, but more than likely y*
Potential to
X* rather than y*
Regardless
Responsibility to
Restitution to x for y
Result of
Sacrifice x* for y*
So x* as to be y*
Subscribe to
Such x* as y* and z*
Think of x* as y*
Use x* as y*

GMAT Insider: Often extra words will be placed between the parts of an idiomatic expression to make it more difficult to identify. In these cases, use the Slash and Burn strategy to isolate the idiom, make sure it is properly constructed, and (if applicable) check that the "x" and "y" are parallel.

A closer look at … Second-Tier Errors

Much like Idiomatic errors, you are best-served to wait until after you have eliminated all other VAMPIRES errors before you check the remaining answer choices for Fluency, Accuracy, and Brevity. However, these errors will often help you make that last decision to correctly choose the right answer.

Consider the previous question regarding the Big Bang. By now, you certainly recognize that the phrase "of all the events" required that we use the idiom "most" and not "more", because there were more than two items. What about the use of the term "maybe"?

The GMAT's preference for Brevity matches with concepts you will learn in business school (and may have learned already). Business writing is expected to be brief, concise, and impactful. Consequently, were you to have arrived at two answers in that question with no distinguishable VAMPIRE errors, but a difference in that one used the phrase "is probably the most difficult" and the other used "is maybe the most difficult", the former would be the correct answer. The term "maybe" connotes very little, whereas "probably" indicates a higher-than-not probability. "Maybe", in a business context, approaches a wasted sentence, and, all other things being equal, the GMAT will demonstrate a strong preference for sentences that do not waste words.

Brevity Tip
When you cannot distinguish grammatical errors between remaining answer choices, look to eliminate answer choices that contain superfluous or redundant words.

8. Experts predict that as many as 100 million species of the world's living organisms remain undetected and unclassified, <u>even considering all the progress made after when *Systema Naturae* was published by Swedish naturalist Carl Linnaeus</u>, the first attempt to classify living organisms using a hierarchical system, in 1735.

(A) even considering all the progress made after when *Systema Naturae* was published by Swedish naturalist Carl Linnaeus

(B) even considering all the progress made after when Swedish naturalist Carl Linnaeus published *Systema Naturae*

(C) even considering all the progress made after Swedish naturalist Carl Linnaeus published *Systema Naturae*

(D) even considering all the progress makes after *Systema Naturae* was published by Swedish naturalist Carl Linnaeus

(E) even considering all the progress made after there being the publishing of *Systema Naturae* by Swedish naturalist Carl Linnaeus

Accuracy

Perhaps more subtle than Brevity errors, Accuracy errors are more definite – test takers often forget to consider the meaning of a sentence in their haste to correct the grammar, but the GMAT occasionally features sentences in which the meaning is illogical, and in these cases the sentence is definitively incorrect.

Accuracy errors often occur when the intent of a sentence is to create a metaphor, but an answer choice is worded in a way that it expresses an actuality.

Example of an accuracy error: *Dumars' game-winning shot gently fell through the net because it had been guided by an angel.*

The same sentence, corrected: *Dumars' game-winning shot gently fell through the net as though it had been guided by an angel.*

In this statement, it is inaccurate to say that the shot was, indeed, guided by an angel. The author is clearly drawing a metaphor, so although the initial sentence has no discernable grammatical flaw, it is definitely incorrect because it is inaccurate.

Accuracy errors can also act similar to Equivalent Elements errors, when a sentence creates a relationship that could not exist.

Example: *Peter thought that the siren on the radio was a police officer approaching behind him.*

The same sentence, corrected: *Peter thought that the siren on the radio was that of a police car approaching behind him.*

As with any Second-Tier error, look for Accuracy errors when you consider remaining answer choices that do not seem to contain any VAMPIRE errors.

9. Already anxious after watching a horror movie, Michele mistook <u>the sound of a backfiring car as the blast of a gunshot</u>.

(A)   the sound of a backfiring car as the blast of a gunshot

(B)   a car as it was backfiring for the blast of a gunshot

(C)   the sound of a backfiring car for the blast of a gunshot

(D)   a car as it was backfiring as the blast of a gunshot

(E)   a backfiring car as the blast of a gunshot

10. The dolphin, one of nature's most intelligent animals, has been known to cover its snout with ocean sponges to better forage for food, <u>in effect creating their own farming equipment</u>.

(A) in effect creating their own farming equipment

(B) so that it creates its own farming equipment

(C) so that they create their own farming equipment

(D) in effect creating its own farming equipment

(E) creating effective farming equipment

Assorted Problems

11.   The question of whether to allocate a portion of their salaries to retirement plans is particularly troublesome for recent college graduates, whose salaries are typically lower <u>than</u> senior members of companies; with the rising cost of living, younger employees often struggle with having to pay bills while trying to save for the long run.

(A)   than

(B)   than those of

(C)   than is so of

(D)   compared to

(E)   compared to those of

12.   Visitors to the zoo have often looked up into the leafy aviary and <u>saw macaws resting on the branches, whose tails trail</u> like brightly colored splatters of paint on a green canvas.

(A)   saw macaws resting on the branches, whose tails trail

(B)   saw macaws resting on the branches, whose tails were trailing

(C)   saw macaws resting on the branches, with tails trailing

(D)   seen macaws resting on the branches, with tails trailing

(E)   seen macaws resting on the branches, whose tails have trailed

13.   In 1971, for the first time in over a century, the value of goods imported to the
       United States <u>was in excess of the value of American goods</u> exported abroad.

(A)   was in excess of the value of American goods

(B)   had an excess over the value of American goods that were

(C)   exceeded the American goods that were

(D)   numbered more than the American goods

(E)   exceeded the value of American goods

14.   Since oil was discovered within the city, the standard of living in Dubai has soared, <u>but the cost of living too</u>.

(A)   but the cost of living too

(B)   and also the cost of living

(C)   but so has the cost of living

(D)   and so also the cost of living

(E)   but so did the cost of living

15.   Surprisingly, it has yet to snow this winter in Salt Lake City, which has forced me to cancel my ski trip to Alta.

(A)   Surprisingly, it has yet to snow this winter in Salt Lake City, which has forced me to cancel my ski trip to Alta.

(B)   Surprisingly, it has not yet snowed this winter in Salt Lake City, which has forced me to cancel my ski trip to Alta.

(C)   What is surprising is that it has yet to snow this winter in Salt Lake City, which has forced me to cancel my ski trip to Alta.

(D)   Surprisingly, it has not yet snowed this winter in Salt Lake City, and I have been forced to cancel my ski trip to Alta.

(E)   Surprisingly, the lack of snow this winter in Salt Lake City had forced me to cancel my ski trip to Alta.

16. <u>Unlike water, which is complimentary</u>, all passengers will need to pay cash for beverages during the transoceanic flight.

(A)   Unlike water, which is complimentary

(B)   Besides water, which is offered free of charge

(C)   Unless the drink is water, which is complimentary

(D)   Not like water, which is offered free of charge

(E)   With water being the only exception

17. Mutual funds, though helpful for personal investors who wish to diversify their portfolios, expose shareholders to additional taxation: <u>not only are taxes on shareholders' eventual sales of the securities collected by the IRS, but also on</u> reinvested dividend stakes earned by the securities held by the fund itself.

(A)   not only are taxes on shareholders' eventual sales of the securities collected by the IRS, but also on

(B)   collected by the IRS are taxes not only on shareholders' eventual sales of the securities, but also on

(C)   taxes not only on shareholders' eventual sales of the securities are collected by the IRS but also

(D)   not only taxes on shareholders' eventual sales of the securities are collected by the IRS, but also on

(E)   taxes are collected by the IRS not only on shareholders' eventual sales of the securities but also

18.   Although breast cancer is only the fifth most common type of cancer, <u>it is so rigorously lobbied that it has become a matter of strong political interest</u> in the United States.

(A)   it is so rigorously lobbied that it has become a matter of strong political interest

(B)   it is of such rigorous lobbying, it has become a matter of strong politic interest

(C)   so rigorously lobbied is it as to become a matter of strong politic interest

(D)   such is its rigorous lobbying, it becomes a matter of strong political interest

(E)   there is so much rigorous lobbying that it has become a matter of strong political interest

19. In 1996 General Electric earned <u>twice as much of its revenue from finance and media operations as they had</u> a decade earlier.

(A) twice as much of its revenue from finance and media operations as they had

(B) double the amount of its revenue from finance and media operations as they did

(C) twice as much of its revenue from finance and media operations as it did

(D) double the amount of its revenue from finance and media operations as it has

(E) twice as much of their revenue from finance and media operations as they had

20.   <u>Over two hundred years ago, Lisa has recently discovered that</u> Jebediah Springfield changed his name to hide his identity after losing a fistfight to George Washington.

(A)   Over two hundred years ago, Lisa has recently discovered that

(B)   Over two hundred years ago, Lisa had recently discovered that

(C)   Lisa has recently discovered that, over two hundred years ago,

(D)   Over two hundred years ago, as Lisa has recently discovered it,

(E)   Lisa has recently discovered, over two hundred years ago, that

21.   Because of dramatic improvements in computing technology, $200 today buys
       <u>double the hard drive space that it has</u> in 2004.

(A)   double the hard drive space that it has

(B)   double the hard drive space that it did

(C)   as much as twice the hard drive space it has

(D)   two times as many hard drive space as there were

(E)   a doubling of the hard drive space that it did

Habits of Great Test Takers: The day before the test, don't do any new problems. Spend a short amount of time reviewing old questions and formulas, and then chill. Watch a movie. Go for a hike. Hang out with friends. In fact, take things a step further and plan out your studying so that you can taper off as the test gets closer, particularly for the last 2 or 3 days. You may think, "I was always great at cramming for tests in school; why shouldn't I go with what works?" The answer: this test is different. The GMAT isn't designed simply to test your knowledge; it's also meant to test your ability to NOTICE things and to find creative solutions. If all you've been doing is studying for hours and days on end, your mind won't be fresh on test day. You'll be trying just to get through the test, to fit everything into easy boxes, and won't be alert to the traps and tricks it tries to throw at you. The most important thing at this stage is having the right mindset – relaxed and focused at the same time.

                                            - Mark Glenn, LOS ANGELES

22. Sir Arthur Conan Doyle's book *The Coming of the Fairies* revealed <u>that this creator of the famous detective Sherlock Holmes, who valued reason above all other qualities, was a spiritualist affected in both his private life and</u> his friend-ships by his belief in psychic phenomena.

(A) that this creator of the famous detective Sherlock Holmes, who valued reason above all other qualities, was a spiritualist affected in both his private life and

(B) that this creator of the famous detective Sherlock Holmes, who valued reason above all other qualities, was a spiritualist and also affected in both his private life and

(C) this creator of the famous detective Sherlock Holmes, who valued reason above all other qualities, was a spiritualist and that he was affected in both his private life and

(D) this creator of the famous detective Sherlock Holmes, who valued reason above all other qualities, was a spiritualist and that he was affected in both his private life as well as

(E) this creator of the most famous detective Sherlock Holmes, who valued reason above all other qualities, to have been a spiritualist and that he affected himself both in his private life as well as

GMAT Insider: As you should recall from Sentence Correction I, when a single verb controls multiple phrases, those phrases must be constructed in the same grammatical form. Parallelism is an important concept on the GMAT and Equivalence errors are very common.

23. When the SARS (Severe Acute Respiratory Syndrome) pandemic occurred in late 2002, officials feared that the outbreak would be widespread; they were concerned that the virus would become a global threat and <u>it would kill vast numbers of patients who would have no protection against it</u>.

(A) it would kill vast numbers of patients who would have no protection against it

(B) it would kill vast numbers of patients with no protection against it

(C) kill vast numbers of patients who would have no protection against it

(D) kill vast numbers of patients who have no protection against them

(E) kill vast numbers of patients with no protection against them

---

GMAT Insider: There are some relative clauses that don't require a pronoun. As long as the relative pronoun would not be the subject of the relative clause, it is acceptable to have no relative pronoun at all. For example, "Matt is not the man he once was" is just as correct as, and is more concise than, "Matt is not the man that he once was."

However, "Jeff went to the town that held the county fair" cannot be rewritten as "Jeff went to the town held the county fair" because "that" is the subject of "held." This distinction is usually obvious when the relative clause is read in context.

24. Buyers at a department store have discovered that the last shipment of towels the store received was subpar in quality; the new towels are <u>slow to dry, not very absorbent, and are</u> harsh and abrasive.

(A) slow to dry, not very absorbent, and are

(B) being slow to dry and not very absorbent, and

(C) slow to dry, not very absorbent, and

(D) slow to dry and not very absorbent, and they are

(E) slow to dry and not very absorbent, and that they are

25. While some politicians propose helping homeowners affected by the housing market downturn by giving them extensive tax breaks, others <u>by opposing the passing of any bailout programs that reward risky lending and borrowing</u>.

(A) by opposing the passing of any bailout programs that reward risky lending and borrowing

(B) by opposing the passage of any bailout programs to reward risky lending and borrowing

(C) oppose the passage of any bailout programs for rewarding risky lending and borrowing

(D) oppose the passage of any bailout programs to reward risky lending and borrowing

(E) oppose passing any bailout programs that reward risky lending and borrowing

26.   Scientific researchers have invested millions of dollars <u>into research to develop</u> <u>more effective treatment for the AIDS virus</u>, including decreasing the drug's side effects and simplifying its regimens of use.

(A)   into research to develop more effective treatment for the AIDS virus

(B)   into research for developing more effective treatment for the AIDS virus

(C)   for research for more effective treatment for the AIDS virus to be developed

(D)   in research to develop more effective treatment for the AIDS virus

(E)   in research for developing for the AIDS virus more effective treatments

27. Having one of the highest melting points of all the chemical elements, tungsten is used in temperature-dependent products such as light bulb <u>filaments so adaptable</u> that it is also used to make wedding bands.

(A) filaments so adaptable

(B) filaments being so adaptable

(C) filaments, yet being so adaptable

(D) filaments, and so adaptable

(E) filaments yet is so adaptable

28.   Turn-of-the-century magician Harry Houdini claimed, <u>for his famous water-torture cell trick, the ability to hold his breath</u> for more than three minutes.

(A)   for his famous water-torture cell trick, the ability to hold his breath

(B)   for his famous water-torture cell trick, he has the ability of holding his breath

(C)   for his famous water-torture cell trick, the ability of him holding his breath

(D)   for his famous water-torture cell trick, to be able to hold his breath

(E)   for his famous water-torture cell trick, being able to hold his breath

29. Experts say that the distribution of counterfeit goods is growing rapidly world-wide, significantly compounding its impact on economic development and copyright infringement, which already are a cost to businesses of several billion dollars per year.

(A) significantly compounding its impact on economic development and copyright infringement, which already are a cost to businesses of

(B) significantly compounding its impact on economic development and copyright infringement, which already cost businesses

(C) significantly compounding its impact on economic development and copyright infringement, already with business costs of

(D) significant in compounding its impact on economic development and copyright infringement, and already costing businesses

(E) significant in compounding its impact on economic development and copyright infringement, and already cost businesses

30. The prehistoric monument Stonehenge is believed to have been erected around 2200 BC, and has attracted the attention of many archaeologists, among them John Aubrey, <u>who believed that the landscape surrounding the site was used by the Druids</u> for religious ceremonies.

(A) who believed that the landscape surrounding the site was used by the Druids

(B) who, believing the landscape surrounding the site was used by the Druids

(C) who, when he had believed that the landscape surrounding the site was used by the Druids

(D) who had believed that the landscape surrounding the site was used by the Druids

(E) believing that the landscape surrounding the site was used by the Druids

31.   The concept of the witch-hunt dates from the fifteenth century, when the
       Church encouraged common citizens <u>should seek out those who were
       suspected to practice sorcery</u>.

(A)   should seek out those who were suspected to practice sorcery

(B)   would do the seeking out of those who were suspected to practice sorcery

(C)   seeking out those who were suspected of practicing sorcery

(D)   the seeking out of those who were suspected of practicing sorcery

(E)   to seek out those who were suspected of practicing sorcery

32.   Perhaps nowhere else in America can one see a greater span of architectural history then on Ivy League campuses with their blend of the classic and the contemporary, <u>each of the campus buildings a monument to the era in which it was</u> built.

(A)   each of the campus buildings a monument to the era in which it was

(B)   all of the campus buildings a monument to the era in which they were

(C)   all of the campus buildings a monument to the era in which it was

(D)   every campus building a monument to the era in which they were

(E)   each of the campus buildings a monument to the era in which they were

33. Art thieves and forgers working together have successfully exchanged carefully crafted reproductions <u>for the famous artists' authentic work, chosen by them</u> to have their masterpieces copied because of the dollar values the paintings can bring.

(A) for the famous artists' authentic works, chosen by them

(B) for the authentic works of famous artists, who were chosen

(C) for the authentic works of famous artists, having been chosen

(D) in place of the famous artists' authentic works, for those of them chosen

(E) in place of the authentic works of the famous artists to have been chosen by them

34. Today's home exercise equipment is typically small and lightweight, allowing fitness buffs to get a complete workout in their own homes while eliminating the need <u>of the requirements of setting aside a large amount of free space and paying for professional installations by older machines</u>.

(A) of the requirements of setting aside a large amount of free space and paying for professional installations by older machines.

(B) of the requirements by older machines of setting aside a large amount of free space and paying for professional installation.

(C) of the requirements for setting aside a large amount of free space and paying for professional installation of older machines.

(D) to pay for professional installation and setting aside a large amount of free space for professional installation, as were required by older machines.

(E) to set aside a large amount of free space and pay for professional installation, as was required by older machines.

35.   From the first-class wait staff to the exotic dishes and the ornate silverware, everything about the banquet <u>was designed to impress, and it is</u>.

(A)   was designed to impress, and it is

(B)   is designed to impress, and it has

(C)   is designed to impress, and it does

(D)   is being designed to impress, and has

(E)   had been designed to impress, and it has

36. James Madison ensured <u>that the United States Constitution conferred specific rights and privileges onto the American people in the text of</u> its first ten amendments, the *Bill of Rights*.

(A) that the United States Constitution conferred specific rights and privileges onto the American people in the text of

(B) that the United States Constitution conferred specific rights and privileges onto the American people because of its text of

(C) the United States Constitution to confer specific rights and privileges onto the American people in its text of

(D) with the United States Constitution that conferred specific rights and privileges onto the American people because it had the text of

(E) with specific rights and privileges that the United States Constitution conferred onto the American people with the text of

37. Intensive diplomatic negotiations led to the war ending almost immediately, when it might have been expected for it to rage for months.

(A) it might have been expected for it to rage for months

(B) it might have been expected to rage for months

(C) it might have been expected that it should rage for months

(D) its raging for months might have been expected

(E) there might have been an expectation it would rage for months

38. A booming population center, the Asian continent is home to over 3.5 billion people, about <u>equivalent to the residents of</u> all the other areas of the world combined.

(A)   equivalent to the residents of

(B)   the equivalent of those residing in

(C)   equal to those who reside in

(D)   as many as the residents of

(E)   as many as reside in

39. <u>At major Hollywood studios, a much greater proportion of the population is
employed than is employed by independent movie production companies.</u>

(A) At major Hollywood studios, a much greater proportion of the population is
employed than is employed by independent movie production companies.

(B) At major Hollywood studios they employ a much greater proportion of the
population than independent movie production companies do.

(C) A much greater proportion of the major Hollywood studios' population is
employed than independent movie production companies employ.

(D) Major Hollywood studios employ a much greater proportion of the population
than the employment of independent movie production companies.

(E) Major Hollywood studios employ a much greater proportion of the population
than independent movie production companies do.

40. Although modern science has essentially eradicated the bubonic plague from the industrialized world, <u>the occasional patient should be diagnosed every few years with the disease</u>.

(A) the occasional patient should be diagnosed every few years with the disease

(B) an occasional patient should be diagnosed with the disease once in every few years

(C) the disease will be diagnosed in the occasional patient once in every few years

(D) every few years the occasional patient will be diagnosed with the disease

(E) every few years the occasional patient should be diagnosed with the disease

41. Independent theaters in Philadelphia have largely abandoned the production of Broadway touring shows and <u>now they often showcase the talents both of local artists who write about local issues and those</u> about broader topics.

(A) now they often showcase the talents both of local artists who write about local issues and those

(B) now often showcase the talents of local artists, both those who write about local issues and those who write

(C) they often showcase the talents of local artists now, both those writing about local issues and who write

(D) often showcase now the talents both of local artists writing about local issues and who are writing

(E) often showcase the talents of both local artists writing about local issues and those

42.   Last year the mean salary of an MBA degree holder was $21,000 more than <u>a person who only held</u> a bachelor's degree.

(A)   a person who only held

(B)   of a person who held only

(C)   that of a person who held only

(D)   a person with only

(E)   those of people who only hold

43.   The Buffalo Club has approved tenets mandating <u>that members should
        volunteer time</u> to aid the community.

(A)   that members should volunteer time

(B)   that time be volunteered by members

(C)   the volunteering of time by members

(D)   members' volunteering of time

(E)   that members volunteer time

44. Additional incentives to teach in the inner cities, <u>such as tuition reimbursement, is</u> giving prospective teachers more to consider when planning where to settle.

(A) such as tuition reimbursement, is

(B) like tuition reimbursement, is

(C) tuition reimbursement being one, is

(D) like tuition reimbursement, are

(E) such as tuition reimbursement, are

45.   <u>Unlike the terms served by Grover Cleveland, separated by four years</u>, all former two-term U.S. Presidents have served consecutive terms.

(A)   Unlike the terms served by Grover Cleveland, separated by four years

(B)   Besides the terms of Grover Cleveland that were separated by four years

(C)   Except for Grover Cleveland, whose terms were separated by four years

(D)   Aside from the terms of Grover Cleveland that were separated by four years

(E)   Other than the separated terms of Grover Cleveland, of four years

46. Setting a precedent that lasted more than a century, George Washington disappointed the people <u>insisting that he should</u> run for a third term as president.

(A)   insisting that he should

(B)   insisting him to

(C)   and their insistence that he

(D)   who insisted that he

(E)   who insisted him to

47.   A new theory proposes that Stonehenge was built to be a monument to the
        dead <u>rather than serving as a giant device that</u> tracked celestial events.

(A)   rather than serving as a giant device that

(B)   rather than a giant device that

(C)   rather than a giant device which

(D)   instead of serving as a giant device that

(E)   instead of a giant device which

48.   Attempts to standardize healthcare, an important issue to both state and
        national officials, has not eliminated the difference in the quality of care
        existing between upper and lower income families.

(A)   has not eliminated the difference in the quality of care existing

(B)   has not been making a difference eliminating the quality of care that exists

(C)   has not made an elimination in the quality of care that exists

(D)   have not eliminated the difference in the quality of care that exists

(E)   have not been making a difference eliminating the quality of care existing

49. A suspect will find it difficult to prove that a police officer used excessive force <u>if there is a lack of some other witness to attest</u>.

(A) if there is a lack of some other witness to attest

(B) unless there will be another witness to attest

(C) without another witness's attestation

(D) should there be no attestation from some other witness

(E) lacking another witness to attest

50.   Lewis Carroll saw children, as other Victorian bachelors, like nuisances rather than beacons of inspiration.

(A)   Lewis Carroll saw children, as other Victorian bachelors, like nuisances rather than

(B)   As did other Victorian bachelors, Lewis Carroll saw children to be a nuisance rather than

(C)   Lewis Carroll saw children to be nuisances, like other Victorian bachelors, rather than seeing them as

(D)   Children to Lewis Carroll, like other Victorian bachelors, were seen as a nuisance rather than

(E)   Lewis Carroll, like other Victorian bachelors, saw children as nuisances rather than

51. According to the Constitution, every person indicted on a crime has the option either to stand trial before a jury or <u>that they simply plead guilty</u> to the crime.

(A) that they simply plead guilty

(B) simply plead their guilt

(C) they should simply plead guilty

(D) should simply plead guilty

(E) to simply plead guilty

52.	In 2003, apartment rental costs in most neighborhoods of Brooklyn rose almost <u>so high, and in certain neighborhoods even higher than what they did</u> in Manhattan.

(A)	so high, and in certain neighborhoods even higher than what they did

(B)	so high, and in certain neighborhoods even higher than, those

(C)	as high, and in certain neighborhoods even higher than, those

(D)	as high as, and in certain neighborhoods even higher than, those

(E)	as high as, and in certain neighborhoods even higher than what they did

53.   If the biologist was correct, the symbiotic relationship of whales and barnacles is
       the result of evolution.

(A)   If the biologist was correct, the symbiotic relationship of

(B)   Should the biologist be correct, the symbiotic relationship of

(C)   If the biologist is correct, the relationship that is symbiotic between

(D)   If the biologist is correct, the symbiotic relationship between

(E)   Should the biologist have been correct, the symbiotic relationship between

54.   <u>A facsimile of Van Gogh's *Starry Night* was so accurately produced that</u> even a group of experienced art appraisers could not distinguish it from the original.

(A)   A facsimile of Van Gogh's Starry Night was so accurately produced that

(B)   So accurately produced was a facsimile of Van Gogh's Starry Night

(C)   It was so accurate that a facsimile of Van Gogh's Starry Night was produced

(D)   A facsimile of Van Gogh's Starry Night that was so accurately produced

(E)   Produced so accurately was a facsimile of Van Gogh's Starry Night that

55.   In the mid-1990's, radical advances in file-sharing software technology allowed users to share music with anyone in the world, <u>changing many people's perceptions of what is considered</u> copyright-protected.

(A)   changing many people's perceptions of what is considered

(B)   changing what many people consider as

(C)   and changed what many people consider as

(D)   and changed many people's perceptions of what is considered

(E)   and it changed many people's perceptions of what is considered as

56.	Laptop computers may be limited in terms of performance, but advocates point out that <u>laptop computers require only half as much as powering desktop computers</u>.

(A)	laptop computers require only half as much as powering desktop computers

(B)	laptop computers require only half as much power as desktop computers do

(C)	powering laptop computers requires only half as much as desktop computers do

(D)	powering laptop computers requires only half as much as it does for desktop computers

(E)	to power laptop computers requires only half as much as for desktop computers

57.   <u>With</u> only 7 percent of the globe's surface area, rainforests contain more than half of the world's plant and animal species, and absorb more carbon dioxide than any other land-based ecosystem on earth.

(A)   With

(B)   As

(C)   Being

(D)   Despite having

(E)   Although accounting for

58.   While earthquakes can threaten most older buildings, <u>they are potentially devastating for solid brick and mortar structures, whose</u> walls – unlike those made of wood – lack the flexibility necessary to withstand shockwaves.

(A)   they are potentially devastating for solid brick and mortar structures, whose

(B)   they can potentially devastate solid brick and mortar structures in that their

(C)   for solid brick and mortar structures they are potentially devastating, because their

(D)   for solid brick and mortar structures, it is potentially devastating in that their

(E)   it can potentially devastate solid brick and mortar structures, whose

59.   A marine biologist predicts that the reintroduction of freshwater fish species into the Thames <u>would fail if the salinity of the water in that river is more numerous than</u> one gram of salt per liter of water.

(A)   would fail if the salinity of the water in that river is more numerous than

(B)   would fail provided the salinity of the water in that river is more than

(C)   should fail if the water salinity in that river was greater than

(D)   will fail if the salinity of the water in that river is greater than

(E)   will fail if the water salinity in that river were more numerous than

60.   In response to concerns about the safety of children in the municipal park, the city council passed an ordinance requiring <u>the owners of dogs over twenty inches in height to be restrained in a leashed harness</u>.

(A)   the owners of dogs over twenty inches in height to be restrained in a leashed harness

(B)   the restraint of owners of dogs over twenty inches in height in a leashed harness

(C)   that owners restrain dogs over twenty inches in height in a leashed harness

(D)   that dogs be restrained over twenty inches in height in a leashed harness by their owners

(E)   dogs to be restrained over twenty inches in height by their owners in a leashed harness

61. Featured in circuses for more than a century, <u>trapeze artists hang from swings by the ankles and perform acrobatic maneuvers, rebalancing frequently enough</u> that spectators see only his continuous, fluid movement.

(A) trapeze artists hang from swings by the ankles and perform acrobatic maneuvers, rebalancing frequently enough

(B) trapeze artists hang from swings by the ankles, they perform acrobatic maneuvers, and with such frequent rebalancing

(C) trapeze artists use their ankles to hang from swings, perform acrobatic maneuvers, and rebalance so frequently that

(D) the trapeze artist hangs from swings by his ankles, performing acrobatic maneuvers and rebalancing so frequently

(E) the trapeze artist hangs from swings by his ankles, performs acrobatic maneuvers, and he rebalances frequently enough

62.   The management proposed <u>that financing for the resort's construction, which could be open to the public early next year, is</u> obtained through a 5-year collateralized bank loan.

(A)   that financing for the resort's construction, which could be open to the public early next year, is

(B)   that financing for the construction of the resort, which could be open to the public early next year, be

(C)   financing for the construction of the resort, perhaps open to the public early next year, to be

(D)   finances for the resort's development, perhaps open to the public early next year, be

(E)   construction financing for the resort, which could be open to the public early next year, is to be

63.   The rapid population growth within the boundaries of the Springfield Public
School District was a source of concern for an overcrowded school system where
the student enrollments of 70 percent of them are above the state board of
education's suggested limits.

(A)   where the student enrollments of 70 percent of them are

(B)   where they have 70 percent of the student enrollments

(C)   where 70 percent of the student enrollments are

(D)   which has 70 percent of the student enrollments

(E)   in which 70 percent of them have student enrollments

64. <u>Deinonychosaurs had a skull that resembled those of the modern birds</u> and so were likely an important evolutionary link between lizard-like dinosaurs and birds alive today.

(A) Deinonychosaurs had a skull that resembled those of the modern birds

(B) Deinonychosaurs had a skull resembling a modern bird's

(C) The skulls of Deinonychosaurs resembled a modern bird's

(D) The Deinonychosaurs' skulls resembled the modern birds'

(E) The skulls of the Deinonychosaurs resembled those of the modern birds

65. After losing a promising deal to a competitor, the sales team was left to reflect on the final day's strange events: the suddenly cold reception with which they were greeted, <u>the offhand gesture that dismissed the proposal's stated benefits, and the cryptic emails received minutes before the presentation</u>.

(A) the offhand gesture that dismissed the proposal's stated benefits, and the cryptic emails received minutes before the presentation

(B) the offhand gesture that dismissed the proposal's stated benefits, and cryptic emails were received minutes before the presentation

(C) the offhand gesture dismissed the proposal's stated benefits, and minutes before the presentation cryptic emails were received

(D) the proposal's stated benefits were dismissed by the offhand gesture, and minutes before the presentation cryptic emails were received

(E) the proposal's stated benefits which were dismissed by the offhand gesture, and cryptic emails that were received minutes before the presentation

Solutions

1. (A)

This question combines Verb and Style issues. In a dependent clause after a verb that expresses demands (such as "require"), the subjunctive mood is necessary. Thus, answers B and C can be eliminated, since even though they both use "require" as a verb, they do not follow with "that" and a verb in the subjunctive mood. Answers D and E use imprecise expressions in place of the verb "require," and do not make clear that the requirement is necessitated by the companies, and can be eliminated. The correct choice, answer A, properly uses the subjunctive "be reviewed," and is clear in its meaning.

2. (C)

The original sentence has a subject-verb agreement error; *Gulliver's Travels* is the title of a book, and is a singular subject, taking a singular verb "was," as choice C correctly states. Choices B and E incorrectly imply that the letter was also published. Choices A and D incorrectly use the conjunction "as" to introduce an adjective clause. The conjunction "as," when introducing a clause, should begin an adverbial clause to explain how or when. The clause modifies a noun, so a relative pronoun -- "that" or "which" -- should begin the clause.

3. (C)

This Modifier question requires that the numerous modifiers in the sentence are organized in a logical fashion. Answer choices A and B incorrectly apply the modifier "originally called BackRub" to the founders of Google, or to two students; in addition to being awkward in nature, either choice applies a singular term, "BackRub" to a plural subject. The modifier "and was originally called BackRub" in answer choice D is at best ambiguous in its reference; most logically, it refers to Dr. Carl Victor Page, incorrectly. Answer choice E incorrectly conjoins a series of modifiers before arriving at a Rudimentary Sentence, "Google was originally called BackRub", and accordingly creates an awkward sentence structure. Answer choice C, the correct answer, logically applies the BackRub modifier to Google, and structures the sentence in a logical, readable manner.

4. (C)

"Politicians and philosophers" is a Modifying phrase that begins this sentence, and must clearly modify the subject of the main clause. Logically, it can only modify "the ancient Greeks", as the modifier is plural and pertains to people. Answer choices A and B both use the modifier to modify early forms of government, which is incorrect. Answer choice D also modifies the forms of government, and not the ancient Greeks, and does so awkwardly using the passive voice and multiple modifiers. Answer choice E is constructed awkwardly using the passive voice, and also contains a Rudimentary Sentence error with the use of the comma in the clause "politicians and philosophers, were the ancient Greeks…". This comma separates the subject and verb, and creates a grammatically incorrect sentence. Only answer choice C, which directly modifies "the ancient Greeks" and does so in a direct way using the active voice, is grammatically correct.

5. (D)

A quick look at the answer choices shows an obvious difference in modification. (A) and (B) start with relative clauses, so students should look before the comma to see if there is noun that can be logically modified by the underlined portion. There is not so (A) and (B) contain modifier errors. Answer choice

(C) contains a rudimentary sentence error as you cannot say The economic data was……, suggests.   (E) uses an appositive modifier which is not precise and contains a redundant and awkward phrase even more…..than even.   (D) uses a participle at the end of the sentence to properly modify the subject of the sentence, economic data, and contains a precise comparison within the modifier.

6. (E)
This Idiom question requires use of the construction, "better served by X **than by** Y." Answer A can be eliminated for using the phrase, "better served by X instead of Y," which is not idiomatically correct. Answer B does not use parallel construction ("selecting… than the selection of") and can also be eliminated for this Equivalent Elements error. Answer C uses the phrase, "better served by X **rather than by** Y," which is not idiomatically correct. Answer D does not use parallel construction ("selecting linemen is better than skill position…") Answer E, the correct choice, properly uses the correct idiomatic construction, "better served by X **than by** Y," and is clear in its meaning.

7. (B)
This question focuses on two Idomatic errors. Because there are multiple events being discussed, the sentence requires "most" and not "more", which would refer to only two events. Thus, answer choices A and D are eliminated. The sentence also requires the infinitive form of the verb "to determine" following "is most difficult", eliminating answer choice C. Answer choice E is awkward and wordy, violating the Fluency and Brevity standards.

8. (C)
This sentence combines Agreement, Idiom and Style elements, and requires that concise and clear wording be used. Answers A and B can be eliminated for incorrectly using the phrase, "after when," which is not idiomatically correct. Answer D can be eliminated for using the present tense "makes," which is not grammatically correct in the context of the sentence. Answer E awkwardly uses the phrase, "made after there being," and can be eliminated for this style error. Also, in answers A, D, and E, the phrasing in the underlined portion makes it appear as though Carl Linnaeus, and not his work Systema Naturae, was the first attempt to hierarchically classify living organisms. The correct choice, answer C, is idiomatically correct, concise, and presents proper subject and verb agreement.

9. (C)
This Idiomatic problem requires the use of the idiom "mistook x for y". Answer choices A, D, and E improperly use the expression "mistook x as y", and are therefore incorrect. Answer choice B is wrong for Accuracy reasons. One cannot mistake an object (a car) for a sound (the blast of a gunshot). In this case, Michele mistook a sound for another sound, as answer choice C correctly connotes.

10. (D)
This Pronoun question requires that the pronoun "its" agree with the singular "dolphin", eliminating answer choices A and C. Answer choices B and E are incorrect because of an Accuracy error. Dolphins aren't actually creating farming equipment, but rather the sentence is offering a metaphor. Answer choice D, which uses the phrase "in effect", properly constructs that metaphor.

Assorted Problem Solutions

11. (B)

This sentence sets up a comparison with the phrase "whose salaries are lower." Answers A and D illogically compare "salaries" with "senior members of companies," and can be eliminated. Answer C can be eliminated for lack of clarity. Answers D and E incorrectly use the redundant phrasing, "lower... compared to." The correct choice, answer B, makes the logical comparison of "salaries" with "those of senior members."

12. (D)

This Tense question requires the correct tense to be used to relate to the present perfect tense ("have looked") in the first predicate of the sentence. Answers A, B, and C incorrectly use the simple past tense ("saw") in the second predicate, and thus can be eliminated for this Tense error. Answer E correctly uses a present perfect tense ("seen") to refer to the "have looked" in the first predicate, but incorrectly uses a present perfect tense "have trailed" with the participle "resting," since this tense does not convey that the tails are trailing at the same time as the macaws are resting; this choice can be eliminated. Also, answers A, B, and E can be eliminated because of a Modifier issue; the modifying phrase cannot begin with the word "whose," since this adjective modifier would logically modify "branches," when it should modify "macaws." The correct choice, answer D, appropriately uses a present perfect tense ("seen") to refer to the first predicate, and a participle ("trailing"). Choice D also fixes the Modifier error; since the modifier begins with "with," it is adverbial and does not need to be next to the word it modifies, "resting."

13. (E)

This Equivalent Elements question requires that the two items being compared – "the value of goods imported" and "the value of American goods exported" – be in the same form. Answer choices C and D incorrectly compare "the value" to "the goods", and are incorrect. Answer choices A and B contain Idiom problems. The clearest, most direct way to express the inequality is to say, as in answer choice E, "the value of X exceeded the value of Y". Accordingly, answer choices E is the correct answer.

14. (C)

This Rudimentary Sentence question requires that the underlined portion exist as an independent clause with its own verb. Answer choices A, B and D each fail to include a verb, and are therefore incorrect. Answer choice E is also incorrect, as it violates the proper Verb Form by using the past tense "did", when the sentence is set in the ongoing present perfect. The verb "has" is required, and answer choice C, the correct answer, uses it properly.

15. (D)

This Modifier problem features the relative pronoun "which", which must modify the word immediately before it. In answer choices A, B, and C, the word "which" is adjacent to "Salt Lake City", which is not what forced the author to cancel the trip. Accordingly, these answers are incorrect. Answer choice E improperly uses the past perfect tense "had" without a past tense event, and is therefore incorrect. Answer choice D, the correct answer, commits neither error, using the connector "and" rather than the modifier "which", and keeping the present perfect tense consistent throughout.

16. (C)

This Modifier problem has as its subject "all passengers", and therefore any modifying phrase must modify passengers. "Water" cannot modify "passengers", and so answer choices A, B, D, and E are all incorrect.

Answer choice C stands out as different because it begins the sentence with an independent clause, "unless the drink is water", which has its own subject and verb, and can therefore stand alone. Accordingly, C is the correct answer.

17. (B)
This Rudimentary Sentence question requires that the word "on" apply to both types of taxes: taxes on shareholders' eventual sales and taxes on reinvested dividend stakes. Answer choices C and E, which do not allow for this necessary connector, are incorrect. Answer choices A and D, though they each include a second occurrence of the word "on", do not use it properly. In each case, the word "on" does not properly connect "taxes" to the reinvested dividend stakes. Answer choice B is tricky, but correct. It properly connects "taxes" to both types of taxable entities with the word "on", but flips the subject and verb at the beginning to distract test-takers. Simply rearranging the subject and verb, you will find that the sentence effectively says: "taxes are collected by the IRS not only on shareholders' eventual sales of the securities, but also on reinvested dividend stakes…". Either this form or the one presented in answer choice B is correct, as the subject-verb order does not change the grammatical correctness of this sentence.

18. (A)
This Idiom and Style sentence focuses on the proper idiomatic construction, "so rigorously lobbied that," and the conciseness and clarity of the sentence. Answers B, D and E use the adjective "lobbying" (rather than the noun "lobbied") and present awkward, wordy phrasing; these answers can be eliminated. Answer C can be eliminated for using the awkward and wordy construction "is it as to become." The correct choice, answer A, properly uses the idiomatic construction, "so rigorously lobbied that," to introduce an explanatory clause.

19. (C)
This question contains a mix of Pronoun, Equivalent Elements, and Verb Form errors. Because General Electric is one, singular entity, the pronouns that refer back to it must also be in the singular form "it". Answer choices A, B, and E, which use the plural "they", are incorrect. The sentence compares the portion of revenue that GE earned in two different time periods, which means that they must be compared in the same form, "earned" to "earned", or "did". Answer choice D fails to do so, using "has" instead, which violates both Equivalent Elements and Verb Form standards, as the event is noted to have taken place in 1986, which is clearly past tense and not present perfect. Accordingly, C, which uses the proper pronoun and equivalent verb form, is correct.

20. (C)
This Verb Form question requires a logical timeline for the sequence of events, which is clearly incorrect in answer choice A; "Lisa has recently discovered" would be a recent event, and not one that took place over two hundred years ago. Answer choice E makes the same mistake, and is also incorrect. In answer choice B, the past perfect "had" is used incorrectly, as the discovery could not have taken place before the event itself. Answer choice D is incorrect, as it uses an unclear pronoun "it" with no clear reference beforehand. Answer choice C, the correct answer, uses the present perfect "has" to indicate a recent discovery, and then properly uses the modifier "over two hundred years ago" to describe Springfield's name change.

21. (B)
This Verb Tense and Modifier problem requires the past tense to be used in the underlined portion (since

it relates to what happened in 2004), an adverb or adverbial phrase to modify the verb "buys," and an un-countable quantifier to refer to the mass noun "hard drive space." Answers A and C can be eliminated for incorrectly using the present tense "has" to state what happened in the past. Answer D incorrectly uses the countable modifier "many," and answer E can be eliminated for lack of clarity. Answer B, the correct choice, properly uses the adverbial phrase "double the hard drive space" to modify the verb "buys" and to refer to a mass noun, and correctly uses the past tense "did."

22. (A)
This sentence combines Idiom and Equivalent Elements components, and requires the phrase, "in both his private life and his friendships" to use parallel structure for the coordinated pair ("both his private life" and "and his friendships"). In the underlined portion, the past participle "affected" modifies the noun "spiritualist," and should be treated as a single, related matter. Answers B, C, D, and E can be eliminated because they all mention "spiritualist" and "affected" separately, treating them as distinct matters. Also, answers B, D, and E make an idiomatic error by using the phrase "as well as" after "both;" and answers C and D omit "that" before the first of two subordinate clauses, failing to use parallel construction. The correct choice, answer A, is idiomatically correct and uses parallel construction.

23. (C)
This sentence combines Pronoun and Equivalent Elements issues, and requires parallel construction and the correct pronoun to refer to the singular "virus." Answers A and B use the phrase, "it would kill," thus creating a new independent clause with the pronoun subject "it," and can be eliminated for lack of parallel structure. Answers D and E can be eliminated for incorrectly using the plural pronoun "them" to refer to the singular antecedent "virus." Answer C, the correct choice, uses parallel verb forms in the relative clause, and a singular pronoun to refer to a singular antecedent.

24. (C)
This Equivalent Elements question requires the use of parallel structure for the four characteristics mentioned: "subpar in quality," "slow to dry," "not very absorbent," and "harsh and abrasive." Answers A, D, and E all repeat the verb "are" before the fourth element ("harsh and abrasive"), and thus do not observe parallel construction and can be eliminated. Answer B uses the word "being," which is awkward and passive, and can be eliminated. The correct choice, answer C, correctly omits the verb "are" before the fourth element and creates parallel structure in the sentence.

25. (E)
This sentence focuses on Equivalent Elements and Style issues, and the correct answer will contain both parallel structure and clear and concise wording. Answers A and B can be eliminated for using a prepositional phrase ("by opposing" and "by borrowing"), while the opening phrase uses a verb ("some propose"); this lacks parallel construction. Answers C and D can be eliminated for using the phrase "the passage," which is stylistically awkward. Answer E appropriately uses parallel construction and is brief and clear; this is the correct choice.

26. (D)
This Idiom and Style question requires usage of the proper preposition (the correct idiomatic construction is "to invest **in**"), and clear phrasing. Answers A and B can be eliminated for using the preposition "into" after "invested," which is idiomatically incorrect. Answer C also uses an incorrect preposition ("for"), and thus can also be eliminated for idiomatic issues. Although answer E uses the correct preposition

("in"), the sentence is awkward ("for developing for the AIDS virus") and can be eliminated for this reason. The correct choice, answer D, uses the idiomatically correct preposition "in" after "invested," and is clear and concise.

27. (E)
This Modifier and Equivalent Elements sentence requires the use of clear wording and parallel construction. Answers A and B can be eliminated because the phrase "so adaptable" should modify "tungsten," not "light bulb filaments." This wording illogically suggests that the "light bulb filaments" are "adaptable," which is not what the sentence intends to state. Answer C can be eliminated because the verb form "being" does not parallel "be used," the first predicate in the clause. Answer D can be eliminated for incorrectly using the conjunction "and" (rather than "yet"), thereby failing to express the contrast. Answer E, the correct choice, properly uses the conjunction "yet," which also correctly links two parallel verb phrases.

28. (D)
This Idiom question requires the use of proper phrasing, and clear, concise construction. Answers A and B do not begin the clause which functions as direct object with the function word "that," and can be eliminated. Answer C uses the unidiomatic phrase, "the ability of him holding his breath," and can also be eliminated. Answer E can be eliminated because it uses the unidiomatic phrase, "claimed being able." The correct choice, answer D, correctly and idiomatically follows the verb "claimed" with the infinitive "to be" to make Houdini's assertion.

29. (B)
This Modifier and Style sentence requires the use of a correct modifier for the verb "is growing," and clear, concise wording. Answer A can be eliminated because the phrase, "are a cost to businesses of," is wordy and indirect. Answer C uses the phrase, "with business cost of," which is wordy and awkward, and can also be eliminated. Answers D and E incorrectly use the adjective "significant," and can be eliminated since an adjective cannot modify the verb "is growing" (the logical referent for the modifying phrase). The correct choice, answer B, appropriately uses "cost" as a verb ("already cost businesses"), which makes the sentence more direct, clear, and concise.

30. (A)
This Tense question requires the correct tense be used to correspond with the simple past verbs "believed" and "attracted" in the original sentence. Answers B and E can be eliminated for incorrectly using the participle "believing," which places the underlined portion in a different tense than the rest of the sentence. Similarly, answers C and E can be eliminated for using the past perfect tense "had believed" instead of the simple past tense "believed." The correct choice, answer A, is the only choice to appropriately use the simple past tense "believed," which corresponds to the original sentence.

31. (E)
This Idiom sentence requires use of the idiomatic construction, "X encouraged Y to do Z." Answers A, B, C, and D all do not follow this construction and produce ungrammatical sentences, and can thus be eliminated. The correct choice, answer E, uses the proper construction, "the Church encouraged common citizens to seek out...," and is idiomatically correct.

32. (A)
This Pronoun and Equivalent Elements sentence uses the uncommon (on the GMAT) set of Equivalent El-

ements called appositive terms—two noun phrases ("each of…" and "a monument") placed next to each other, with one further explaining the meaning of the other. These terms should be parallel and agree in number. Answers B and C incorrectly use the plural "all" with the singular "monument." The pronoun subject + verb of the final clause "it was / they were built" must agree in number with its referent, the singular "each." Only answer A keeps both phrases in the appositive parallel and correctly uses the singular "it was."

33. **(B)**
This sentence uses an idiomatic construction "exchanged x for y." Answers D and E incorrectly complete the idiom with "in place of", instead of "with." Answers A and D use the possessive "artists'", making the sentence awkward and the meaning unclear. Finally, the end of this sentence must be logically connected to the main clause. Answer choices A, C, D, and E use ungrammatical and awkward connectors, and answers A, D, and E use the unnecessary pronoun "them", which has an ambiguous referent. Only answer B uses the idiom correctly, expresses the meaning of the original sentence in a clear and concise manner, and grammatically connects the end of the sentence to the main clause using the relative pronoun "who", while eliminating other unnecessary and unclear pronouns.

34. **(E)**
The end of this sentence contrasts the needs of older machines to those of newer machines. The phrase "the need of the requirements", found in answers A, B, and C, is redundant and unidiomatic. The phrase "**requirements of** older machines" or "**required by** older machines" should not be broken apart. Answer D uses the infinitive "to pay" and the non-parallel participial "setting", creating an Equivalent Elements error: these verbs should be part of a compound predicate, but when their forms are not parallel, as in choice D, it appears that "setting aside… free space" is parallel to "professional installation", making a list of two things that were paid for, which changes the meaning of the original sentence while also being grammatically unsound. Only answer E correctly uses a compound predicate with equivalent elements while avoiding the redundant phrase "the need of the requirements" and keeping each concept logically distinct but connected to the other elements of the sentence.

35. **(C)**
The final clause of this sentence contains a helper or auxiliary verb (e.g. "is", "has", "does") but omits the main verb "impress." For this to be an acceptable grammatical form, the main verb has to fit into the final clause **without** changing form. Answer A requires the noun "impressive." Answers B, D and E require the past participle "impressed." Additionally, answer choice E uses the wrong Verb Form (the past perfect tense) for the main clause, as this clause is not being used to describe an event that occurred previous to **another** event in the past. Only the correct answer, C, uses an appropriate verb form in the main clause and an auxiliary verb "do" in the final clause that fits with "impress."

36. **(A)**
Answers A and B correctly use the relative pronoun "that" to begin the relative clause that acts as the direct object of the verb ensured, while answer C incorrectly omits the word. Answers D and E insert a prepositional "with" phrase before the relative clause, which changes the meaning of the sentence. Answer D also contains a Rudimentary Sentence error ("ensured with x that y" requires parallel structure of equivalent elements). Answer B's phrase, "conferred x because of its text of its… amendments" is unidiomatic, wordy, and confusing; it also introduces a Pronoun error through its use of "its text", which most clearly refers back to "the American people" but should refer to "the… Constitution." Only answer A uses

a grammatical relative clause as the direct object of the verb "ensured", and logically and unambiguously connects the underlined portion to the end of the sentence.

37. (B)

The end of this sentence is a subordinate clause introduced by "when", and uses the subjunctive "might have been" to describe an expected reality that is contrary-to-fact. Answers A and C use unidiomatic constructions to describe the expectation ("expected for it to rage", "expected that it should rage.") Answers D and E create constructions that can be eliminated as Style errors (the awkward "its raging for months" as subject of the subordinate clause; the very passive "there might have been an expectation" which should be followed by "that"). Only answer B uses a concise and correct idiom with the subordinate "when" clause.

38. (E)

The comparative phrase of this sentence is meant to suggest that there are approximately 3.5 billion people living outside of the Asian continent. Answers A, B, and C use comparative terms with meanings that are too broad; in the context of countable things (such as people), "equivalent to/of" and "equal to" suggest a similarity between the two groups being compared that is beyond the scope of this question. These two phrases would be more appropriate for a comparison between **uncountable** things, such as in the sentence, "The amount of water spilled on the floor was about equal to the amount left in the pitcher." Answer D's comparative phrase "3.5 billion people [is] as many as the residents" is unidiomatic, and stylistically awkward. Answer E correctly uses the "as many as" idiom for its comparative phrase, and concisely words the comparison to clearly compare people in Asia to people in other areas of the world.

39. (E)

Answer A begins with the absolute phrase, "At major Hollywood studios", which grammatically modifies the entire sentence; separating this information from the comparative clause illogically suggests that more people are "employed than... employed" by independent companies. Answer B uses the pronoun "they" with an unclear antecedent; the beginning of this sentence either means the redundant "At major studios, major studios employ" or "At major studios, [some plural nouns] employ", using a pronoun with no antecedent. Answer C uses the passive "is employed" and the active "employ" for the two halves of the comparative main clause, and can be eliminated for not using parallel structure among equivalent elements; answer C additionally changes the meaning of the original sentence, suggesting that the population **of** studios **is** employed, rather than that the population **is** employed **by** studios. Answer D uses the present tense verb "employ" and the noun form "employment" for the two halves of the comparative main clause, a failure to use parallel structure. Only answer E correctly uses parallel structure of equivalent elements ("employ" and "do") while clearly expressing the meaning of the original sentence.

40. **(D),** In answer A, the order of the phrases "every few years" and "with the disease" that modify "diagnosed" illogically suggest that the **same** patient is being diagnosed with the disease every few years. In answers A, B, and E, the auxiliary verb "should" is used to describe a future situation; this usage suggests that the speaker believes that this diagnosis **ought** to happen, and should be eliminated. Answers B and C use the temporal phrase "once in every few years", which is unidiomatic and stylistically awkward. Only answer D uses "will", an appropriate auxiliary to describe a predicted (but not sought-after) future situation, while idiomatically expressing its temporal phrase in a way that keeps the intent of the original sentence clear.

41. (B)
Answers A and C use the pronoun "they" as the subject of the verb "showcase", creating a second independent clause in this sentence; without a comma before the conjunction "and", this creates an ungrammatical Rudimentary Sentence error (in the form of run-on sentences). Answers C and D fail to use parallel structure (C: "both **those writing**…and **who write**" and D: "both **of local artists writing** …and **who are writing**"). Answer E suffers from a Style error due to the ambiguous placement of "both"; this sentence could suggest that there are exactly two local artists writing about local issues, both of whom are showcased by independent theaters. Only answer B correctly makes "showcase" the second verb in a compound predicate "theaters… have abandoned… and now… showcase"), uses a clear placement of the word "both", and maintains parallel structure among equivalent elements.

42. (C)
The equivalent elements sentence requires the comparison with the "mean salary" to be logical, so Answer A ("a person") can be eliminated, Answer B ("of a person") can be eliminated, and Answer D ("a person") can be eliminated. The "mean salary" is a singular idea, so answer E, which uses the plural pronoun "those," makes it sound as though there is more than one mean salary. Answer E can therefore be eliminated for the Pronoun error. The correct answer choice, C, logically compares "mean salary" to the singular pronoun "that."

43. (E)
The participle "mandating" sets up an idiomatic construction that can follow two alternative forms: either "mandating that N V" or "mandating N to V," where N is the noun subject and V is the unconjugated form of the verb. The original sentence follows the first idiomatic form, but unnecessarily includes the helper verb "should." Answer A can be eliminated for the Idiomatic error. Answer B ("that time be volunteered by members") makes the sentence passive by treating "time" as the subject not "members," and B can be eliminated for this reason. Answer C ("the volunteering of time by members") fails to follow either idiomatic construction and can be eliminated for the Idiomatic error. Answer D ("members' volunteering of time") fails to use either idiomatic construction and can be eliminated for the Idiomatic error. Answer E ("members to volunteer time") correctly uses the "mandating N to V" construction and is the correct answer.

44. (E)
The Agreement problem in the sentence requires that a plural verb be used with the plural subject "incentives." Answers A, B, and C all use "is" and can be eliminated for the Agreement error. The use of "like" in Answer D sets up an illogical and unintentional comparison between "incentives" and "tuition reim-bursement." Answer D can be eliminated for the Equivalent Elements error. Answer E correctly uses the verb "are" and the correct expression "such as" to introduce an example of the "incentives." Answer E is the correct choice.

45. (C)
Answers A, B, D, and E all make an illogical comparison between "the terms" and "Presidents" and can be eliminated for the Equivalent Elements error. Answers B and D also use the modifying phrase "that were separated by four years" in a way that makes it sound as though Cleveland had other terms that were not separated by four years. Both answers can be eliminated for the Modifying error. Answer E places the modifying phrase "of four years" nowhere near the noun "terms" and can be eliminated for the Modify-ing error. Answer C correctly compares "Grover Cleveland" to "Presidents," uses the modifier "which were

separated by four years" to correctly modify "terms," and is the right choice.

46. (D)

The verb "insist" needs to be followed by the preposition "that" to be idiomatic, so answers B ("insisting him") and E ("insisted him") can be eliminated for the Idiomatic errors. Answer C makes it sounds as if Washington disappointed "their insistence" as well as "the people," and can be eliminated for its awkward and confusing construction. Answer A uses the unnecessary helper verb "should" and can be eliminated for the Redundancy error. Answer D correctly uses the idiom "insisted that" and is the right choice.

47. (B)

The word "which" needs to follow a comma when it is used to describe or elaborate on an idea, and since "which" does not follow a comma in Answers C and E, they can be eliminated. Answers A and D lack the parallel construction needed to make a comparison. The parallel construction, "was built as X rather than Y," is required for proper form. A and D offer "serving as a...." as the second half of a comparison that begins with the noun "a monument". This Equivalent Elements error allows A and D to be eliminated. Answer B compares "a monument" with "a giant device" in correct parallel fashion, and is the right choice.

48. (D)

This Agreement and Style problem requires that a plural verb be used to modify the plural subject "attempts," and the sentence be concise and neither ambiguous nor awkward. Answers A, B, and C can be eliminated for incorrectly using the singular verb "has" to modify the plural subject "attempts." Answer E muddles the meaning of the sentence, and can be eliminated for lack of clarity. Thus, the answer D is the correct choice, because it appropriately uses the plural verb "have," and is concise and grammatically sound.

49. (C)

This question focuses primarily on Style issues, and the correct sentence needs to be clear and concise. Answers A and D are awkward and wordy (both use a wordy inverted clause, beginning with "there"), and can be eliminated. Answer B incorrectly uses the future tense "will be" after a result clause that uses the future tense "will find," and can be eliminated for this reason. Answer E uses the participle "lacking," which introduces a dangling modifier, since the "lacking…" phrase cannot logically modify "force," the nearest noun. The correct choice, answer C, uses a prepositional phrase that conveys the meaning of the sentence efficiently and idiomatically.

50. (E)

This Idiom question requires the use of the proper idiom "saw children as…" in the correct sentence. Answer A can be eliminated for incorrectly using the phrase "as other Victorian bachelors," which lacks a verb, and thus is not grammatically parallel with the opening clause. Answers B and C use the unidiomatic construction "saw children to be," and can be eliminated for the idiomatic error. Answer D uses a confusing and awkward passive construction, and can be eliminated for the lack of clarity. Answer E properly uses the idiomatic construction "saw children as," and is the correct choice.

51. (E)

This Equivalent Elements question requires the use of parallel construction between the two clauses in the sentence. Answers A, B, C, and D fail to use the infinitive after the second clause, and thus the underlined portion in each of these choices does not correspond with the infinitive used in the unchanged

portion of the sentence ("to stand trial"), and can be eliminated for this Equivalent Elements error. Answer E, the correct choice, uses the infinitive "to," and therefore appropriately creates parallel construction with the unchanged part of the sentence.

52. (D)
This Idiom and Equivalent Elements question requires the use of the idiomatically correct expression, "as high as," and parallel construction in the underlined portion of the sentence. Answers A and B can be eliminated for using "almost so high," which is an idiomatic error. Answer C also commits an idiomatic error by using the phrase "almost as high," instead of the correct "almost as high as." Answer E, like A, does not end the parenthetical comment with a comma, and thus fails separate the parenthetic expression; this can be eliminated for its Equivalent Elements error. The correct choice, answer D, appropriately uses the idiom, "as high as," and encloses the parenthetical comment "and in certain neighborhoods… than" in commas.

53. (D)
This Verb Form and Idiom question requires the use of the proper tense, and the correct idiomatic construction "relationship between X and Y" in the sentence. Answers A, B, and E can be eliminated for failing to use the present indicative in the conditional clause (to correlate with the present tense "is" used in the main clause). Answers A and B also incorrectly use the unidiomatic phrase "relationship of," and thus can also be eliminated for the idiomatic error. Answer C includes an unnecessary additional clause ("that is symbiotic"), and can be eliminated for wordiness. Answer D correctly uses the present indicative in the conditional clause, and uses the correct idiomatic construction "relationship between X and Y;" this is the correct answer.

54. (A)
This Equivalent Elements question requires the subordinate clause at the end of the sentence to be introduced with the word "that," to set up a logically and grammatically correct phrase. Answers B, C, and D fail to do this, and can be eliminated for having an Equivalent Elements error. Answer C begins the sentence with a pronoun without a referent ('it'), and can be eliminated. Answer A appropriately sets up the unchanged portion of the sentence as a result clause, introducing it with the subordinating conjunction "that," and thus is the correct choice.

55. (A)
This Idiom and Style question requires the correct sentence to be concise, clear, and idiomatically correct. Answers B, C, and D include the preposition "as" (meaning "in the capacity of") after the verb "considered," which is not idiomatically correct, and can be eliminated. Answer E distorts the meaning of the sentence by making "changed" a separate action, and can be eliminated for lack of clarity. The correct choice, answer A, correctly omits the unnecessary preposition "as," and is clear and to the point.

56. (B)
This Equivalent Elements question requires parallel construction between the comparisons used in the sentence. Answers A, C, D, and E all make illogical comparisons and can be eliminated (answer A compares "laptop computers" with "powering laptop computers," answer C compares "powering laptop computers" with "desktop computers," answer D compares "powering laptop computers" with "it does for desktop computers," and answer E compares "to power laptop computers" with "for desktop computers"). The correct choice, answer B, is the only answer that correctly makes a logical comparison ("laptop

computers" with "desktop computers"), and that uses parallel grammatical structure for the comparison (the verb "require" with "do").

57. (E)
This sentence should begin with a phrase that sets up a contrast between the size of the rainforest and its disproportionate representation in biodiversity and carbon absorption. The original sentence does not establish this contrast and neither does answer choice B or C. Answer choices D and E, however, do establish this contrast. The beginning of the original sentence ("With only 7 percent…") confusingly suggests that rainforests somehow possess, rather than constitute, 7 percent of the world's surface area. Answer choice D also contains this error. The remaining answer, choice E, does establish the contrast and clearly states that rainforests constitute 7 percent of the globe's surface area.

58. (A)
In the original sentence, the plural pronoun "they" agrees in number with its antecedent "earthquakes." The possessive pronoun "whose" clearly refers to "structures" and effectively connects them to the idea of vulnerability. Answer choices B and E use the redundant wording "can potentially." Answer choices B and D link to the end of the sentence with "in that their"; answer choice C links with "because their." Since the antecedent for "their" might be either "they" or "structures," answer choices B, C, and D can be eliminated for the pronoun errors ("P"). These answers are also unnecessarily wordy. Answer choices D and E incorrectly use the singular pronoun "it" after the plural antecedent "earthquakes." Answer choice A correctly begins the main clause with a plural pronoun, and effectively links to the end of the sentence with the pronoun "whose." Thus, answer choice A is the correct answer.

59. (D)
The original sentence presents three related clauses: 1) "…biologist predicts"; 2) "that…reintroduction… would fail"; and 3) "if…salinity is…" The conditional "would fail" in the "that" clause is inconsistent with the present indicative verbs in the main and "if" clauses. This is a failure to use the correct verb form ("V"). The original sentence uses the adjective "numerous" to quantify the uncountable noun "salinity," and hence commits a modifier error ("M"). Answer choice B, like A, incorrectly uses the conditional "would fail" in the "that" clause and the present indicative "is" in the "if clause." Answer choice C incorrectly uses "should fail" in the "that" clause and the past tense "was" in the "if" clause. Answers choices D and E both use the future indicative "will fail" in the "that" clause, but in the "if" clause, answer choice E incorrectly uses the subjunctive "were" in the "if" clause. Answer choice D correctly uses the present indicative "is." Answer choice B inappropriately uses the word "more" to quantify "density;" answer choices E and A use the adjective "numerous." Only answer choice D uses a correct sequence of present and future indicative verb forms – "predicts," "will fail," and "is" – in the three related clauses, and thus it is the correct answer choice.

60. (C)
The answer to this question must accurately express the meaning of the city council's dog ordinance. The original sentence absurdly indicates that owners, not dogs, are to be restrained, as does answer choice B. Answer choices D and E place "over twenty inches in height" so it appears to modify "restrained." Answer choice E also places "in a leashed harness" so it appears to modify "owners." Answer choice C most accurately and efficiently expresses the meaning of the ordinance, and is the correct answer.

61. (D)
The end of the sentence uses the singular possessive pronoun "his." Since this portion of the sentence is

unchanging, the antecedent for the pronoun must also be singular so it agrees in number. The original sentence incorrectly uses the plural "artists," which constitutes a pronoun error ("P"). Answer choices B and C also make the mistake of using the plural "artists," whereas answer choices D and E use the singular "artist." The original sentence and answer choice E both use the phrase "frequently enough that," which is an idiomatic error ("I"). The proper idiomatic expression is "so frequently that." Answer choice B does not properly use equivalent elements ("E") in its series "artists hang…, they perform,…and with…" Likewise, answer choice E improperly uses the series "artist hangs…, performs…, and he rebalances…" Answer D correctly uses the singular "artist" and the idiomatic phrase "so frequently that." Answer choice D alone subordinates "performing" and "rebalancing" to "hangs…by his ankles," recognizing that the trapeze artist does not descend from the swings in order to perform acrobatic maneuvers (at least intentionally!). Answer choice D is correct.

62. (B)
Following the verb "proposed," the verb in the dependent clause must be in the subjunctive mood. The original sentence incorrectly uses the indicative "is." Also in that sentence, the relative clause "which could be open…" modifies "construction" rather than "resort," creating a modifier error ("M"). Answer D makes this mistake as well. Answer choices A, C, and E do not use the correct form of the verb "be" in the dependent clause. Answer choices C, D, and E fail to introduce the dependent clause with "that." This omission gives the impression that the management proposed financing, not the manner in which the finances would be obtained; C, D, and E can therefore be eliminated for lack of clarity. Answer choices B and D both correctly use the subjunctive verb "be" in the dependent clause, but only answer choice B avoids potential confusion by introducing the dependent clause with the conjunction "that." Thus, answer choice B is the correct answer.

63. (C)
In the original sentence, the pronoun "them" has no stated antecedent, so this answer presents a pronoun error ("P"). The implied referent for the pronoun "them" is the [concerned members of the] school system, yet the statistic applies to the school enrollments, so this wording suffers from a lack of clarity. Answer choice B uses the pronoun "they" without a stated antecedent. Similarly, answer choice E uses the pronoun "them" without a stated antecedent (in the same way that answer choice A does). Answer choices B (with "have") and D (with "has") use wording that suggests the school system possesses 70% of all student enrollments above the state limits, and should be eliminated for lack of clarity. Only answer C uses a clear, direct, and economical adjective clause to indicate the percentage of student enrollments above the state limits in the school system in question. Thus, answer C is correct.

64. (B)
The unchanging portion of this sentence provides the second half of a compound predicate, and the original sentence logically uses "Deinonychosaurs" as subject for both halves ("had a skull," "and so were…"). In the original sentence, the pronoun "those" does not agree in number with its antecedent "skull," so this wording commits a pronoun error ("P"). Answer choice B, like A, logically makes "Deinony-chosaurs" subject of the compound predicate. Answer choices C, D, and E make "skulls" subject of the compound predicate. Answer choice B states "a skull resembling a modern bird's," and is thus grammatically correct and the correct answer choice.

65. (A)
The unchanging portion of the sentence ends with a colon followed by the first item in a series: "…

strange events: the suddenly cold reception with which they were greeted…" This first item establishes the form that other members of the series must follow to maintain equivalent elements. The original sentence continues the series with noun phrases ("the offhand gesture…" and "the cryptic emails") which do follow the grammatical structure of the first item. Additionally, the original sentence begins each noun phrase with "the," following the form of the first item. Answer choices D and E illogically begin the second item with "the proposal's stated benefits," rather than the strange event ("the offhand gesture"), and can be eliminated for lack of clarity. Answer choices B, C, D, and E can be eliminated because they fail to maintain parallel structure in the coordinate series of the three strange events. Only answer A correctly uses noun phrases introduced by "the" for the second and third members of the series ("the offhand gesture…" and "the cryptic emails"), and thus it is the correct answer.

Answer Key

Lesson

1 . . . . A
2 C
3 C
4 C
5 . . . . . . D
6 . . . . . . E
7 . . . . . . B
8 C
9 C
10 . . . . . D

Drill

1 . . . . S
2 . . . . S
3 . . . . S
4 . . . . S
5 . . . . P
6 . . . . S
7 . . . . P
8 . . . . . . S
9 . . . . S
10 . . . . . S
11 . . . . . S
12 . . . . . S
13 . . . . . S
14 . . . . . P
15 . . . . . S

Assorted

11 . . . . . B
12 . . . . . D
13 . . . . . E
14 C
15 . . . . . D
16 C
17 . . . . . B
18 . . . . . A
19 C
20 C
21 . . . . . B
22 . . . . . A
23 C
24 C
25 . . . . . E
26 . . . . . D
27 . . . . . E
28 . . . . . D
29 . . . . . B
30 . . . . . A
31 . . . . . E
32 . . . . . A
33 . . . . . B
34 . . . . . E
35 C
36 . . . . . A
37 . . . . . B
38 . . . . . E
39 . . . . . E

40 . . . . . D
41 . . . . . B
42 C
43 . . . . . E
44 . . . . . E
45 C
46 . . . . . D
47 . . . . . B
48 . . . . . D
49 C
50 . . . . . E
51 . . . . . E
52 . . . . . D
53 . . . . . D
54 . . . . . A
55 . . . . . A
56 . . . . . B
57 . . . . . E
58 . . . . . A
59 . . . . . D
60 C
61 . . . . . D
62 . . . . . B
63 C
64 . . . . . B
65 . . . . . A

THE MBA TOUR

Your future begins here

The MBA Tour offers Quality Interaction With Top Business Schools

MEET with school representatives at our OPEN FAIR

LISTEN to top school experts discuss valuable MBA admission topics at our PANEL PRESENTATIONS

DISCUSS individual school qualities with representatives at our ROUNDTABLE EVENTS

ASIA
TOKYO

SEOUL

TAIPEI

BEIJING

SHANGHAI

BANGKOK

SINGAPORE

INDIA
BANGALORE

NEW DELHI

MUMBAI

UNITED STATES
HOUSTON

CHICAGO

ATLANTA

NEW YORK

BOSTON

WASHINGTON DC

LOS ANGELES

SAN FRANCISCO

SOUTH AMERICA
BUENOS AIRES

SANTIAGO

SAO PAULO

LIMA

BOGOTA

MEXICO CITY

EUROPE
MUNICH

LONDON

PARIS

CANADA
CALGARY

VANCOUVER

TORONTO

MONTREAL

Register at www.thembatour.com

THE MBA TOUR
Your future begins here